MW00946963

Published By

Lawyer Coloring Book Publishing

LAWYER
NOT A MAGICIAN
BUT I UNDERSTAND
YOUR CONFUSION

ONLY JUDY
CAN JUDGE ME

LAWYER
BY DAY
REAL TIRED
BY NIGHT

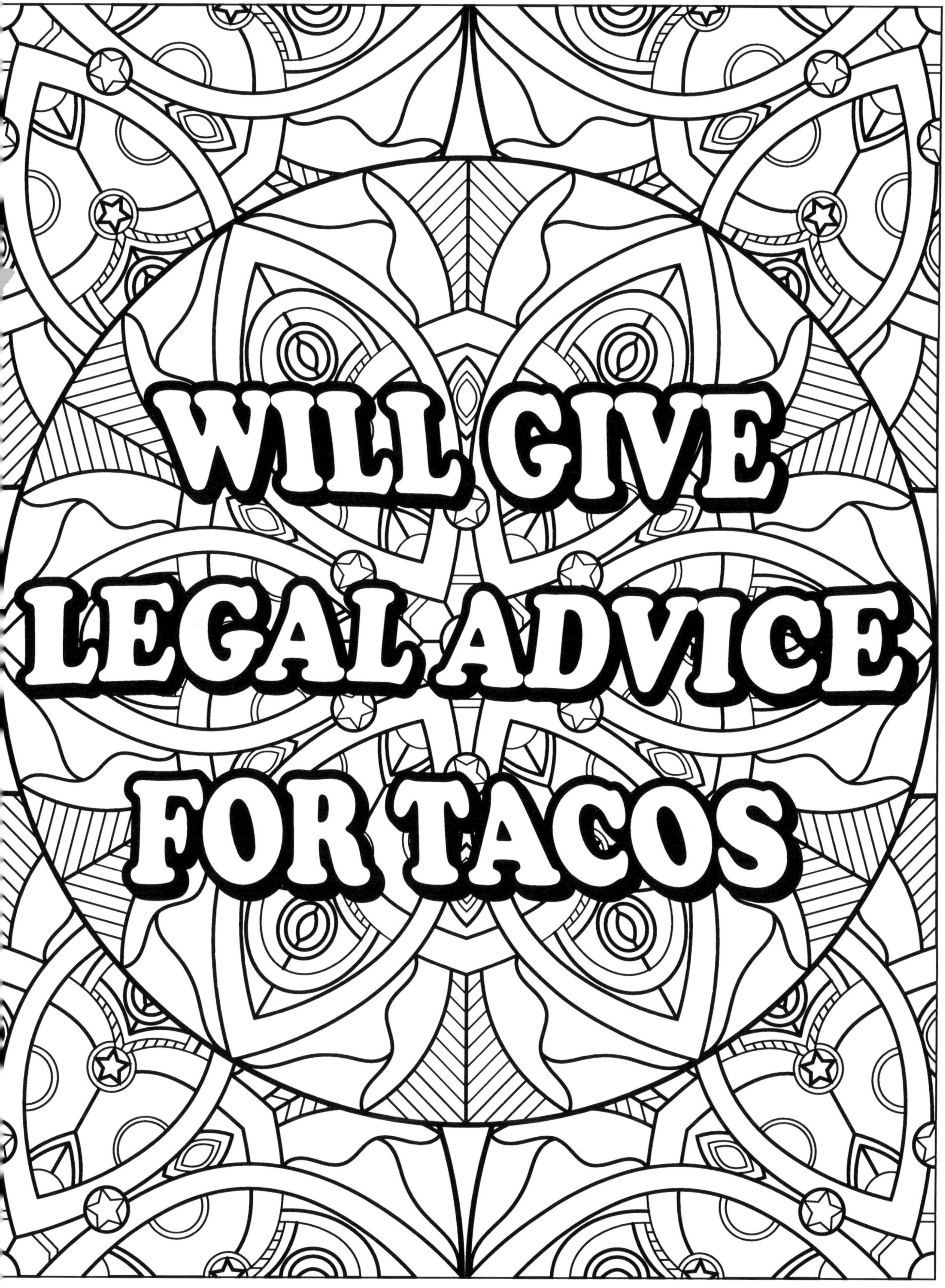
WILL GIVE
LEGAL ADVICE
FOR TACOS

I'M A LAWYER
TO SAVE TIME
LET'S ASSUME
I'M ALWAYS
RIGHT

I COULD BE A
MOVIE STAR
BUT DECIDED TO
BECOME A
LAWYER INSTEAD

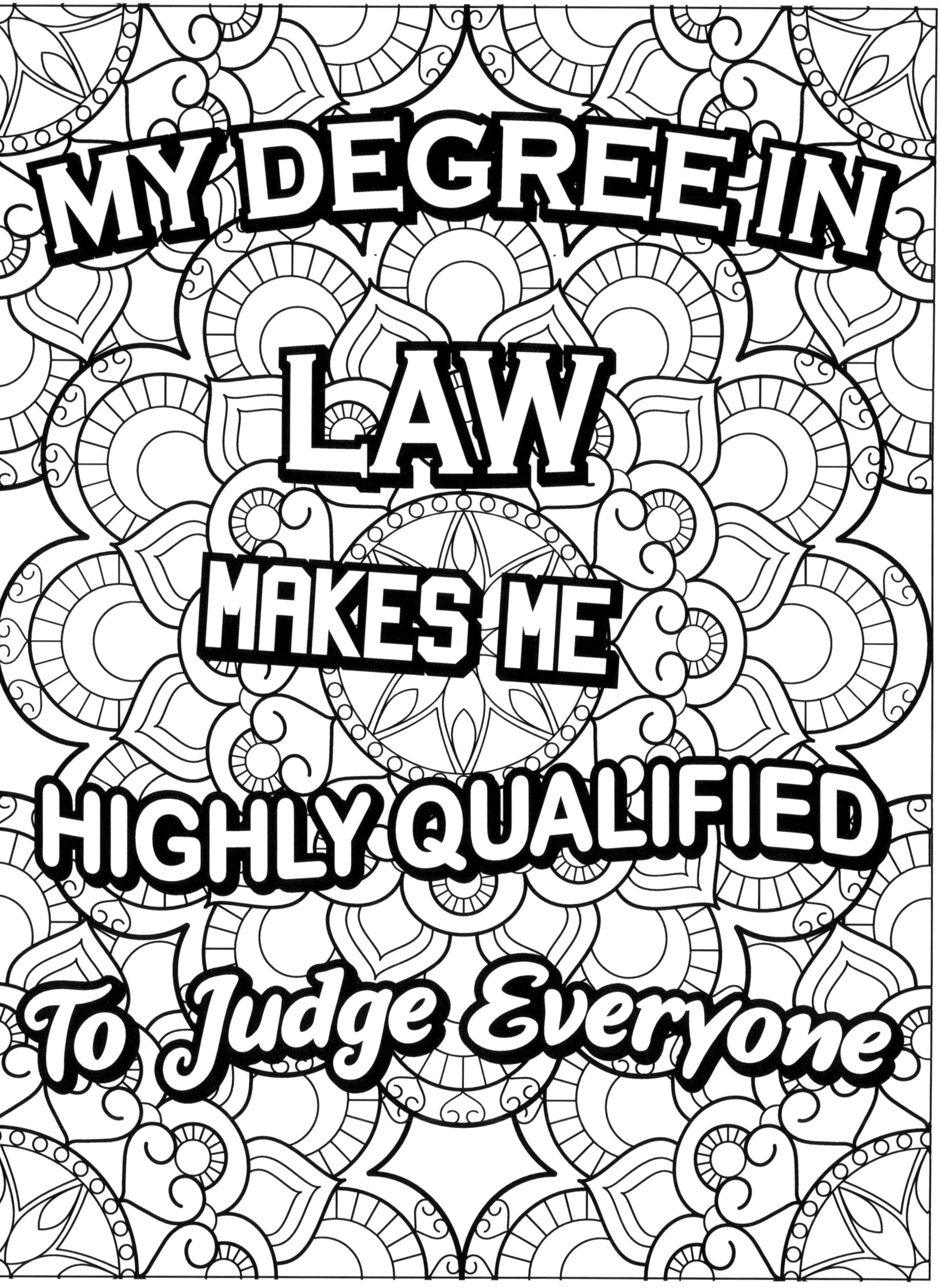
MY DEGREE IN
LAW
MAKES ME
HIGHLY QUALIFIED
To Judge Everyone

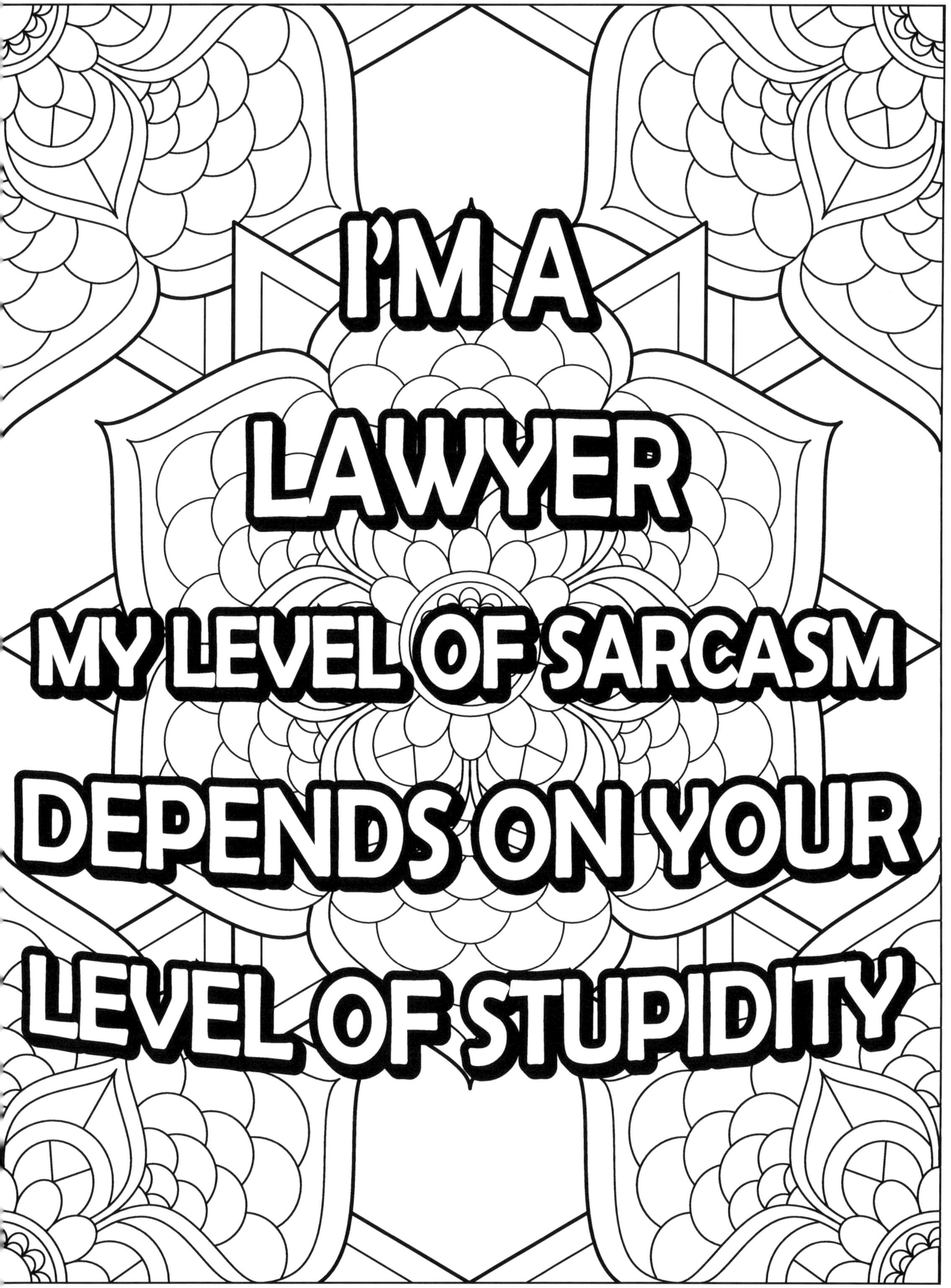
I'M A
LAWYER
MY LEVEL OF SARCASM
DEPENDS ON YOUR
LEVEL OF STUPIDITY

I'M NOT ARGUING
I'M JUST EXPLAINING
WHY I'M RIGHT

DON'T ARGUE
WITH THE
LAWYER

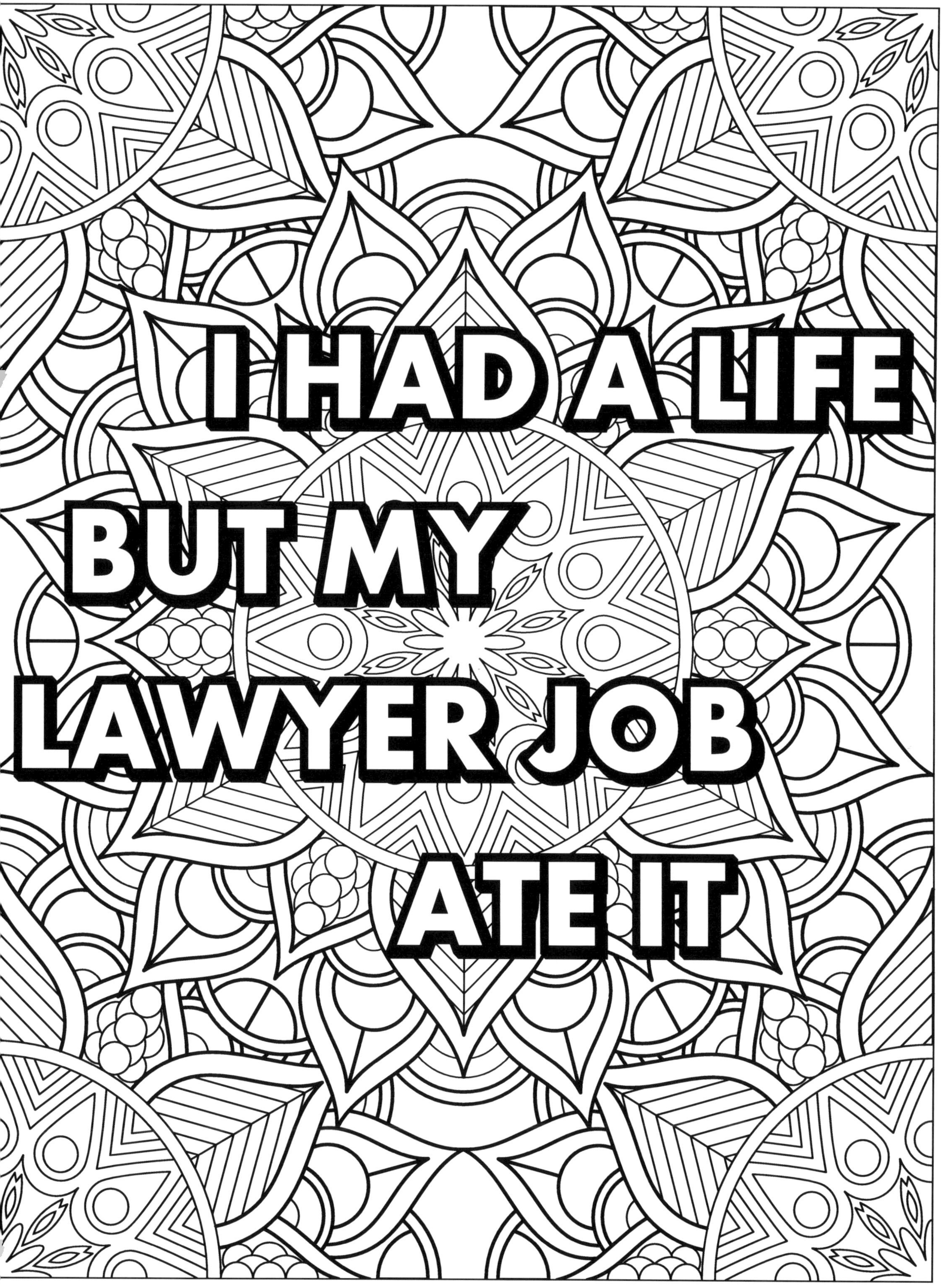
I HAD A LIFE
BUT MY
LAWYER JOB
ATE IT

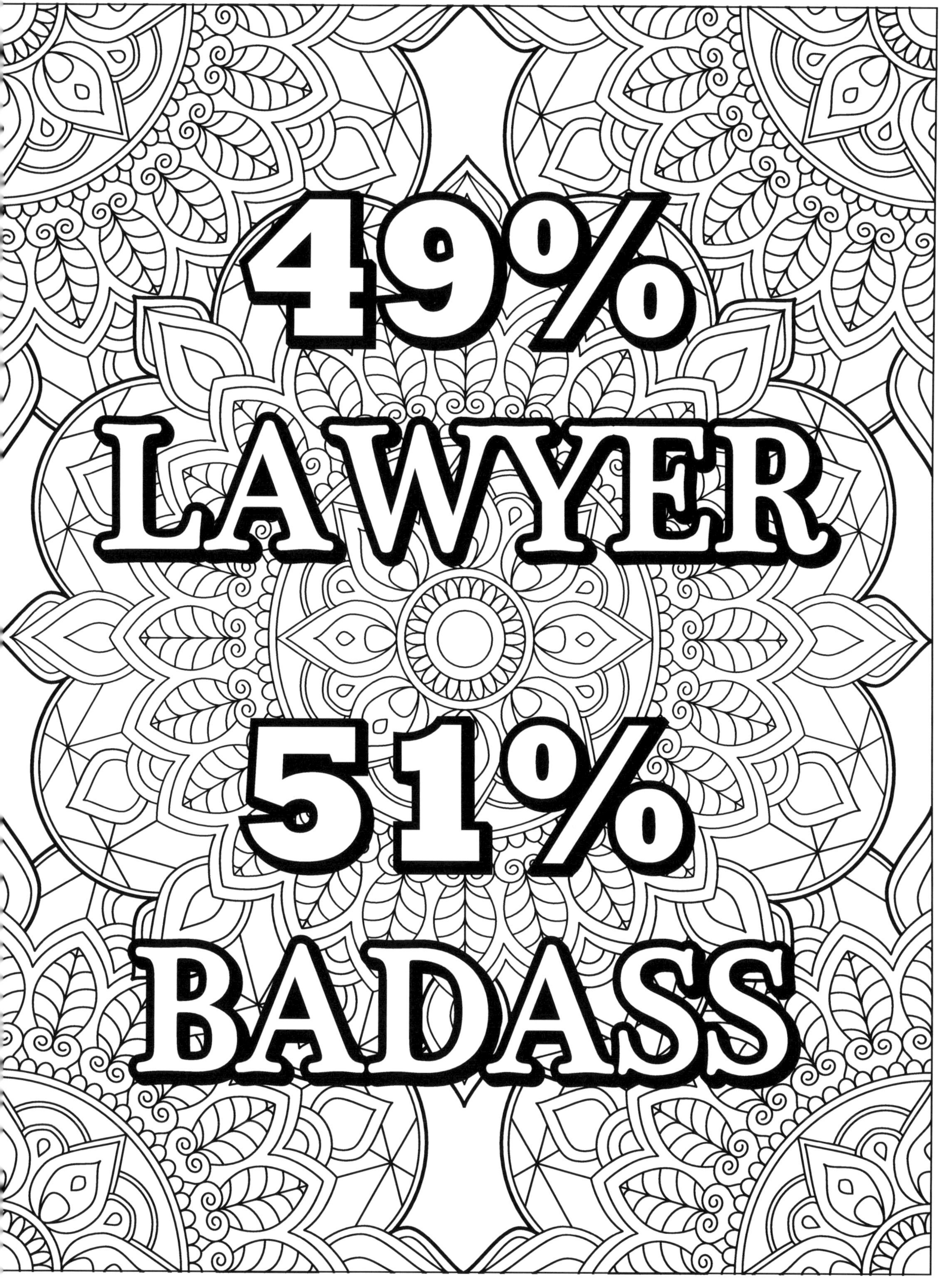
49%
LAWYER
51%
BADASS

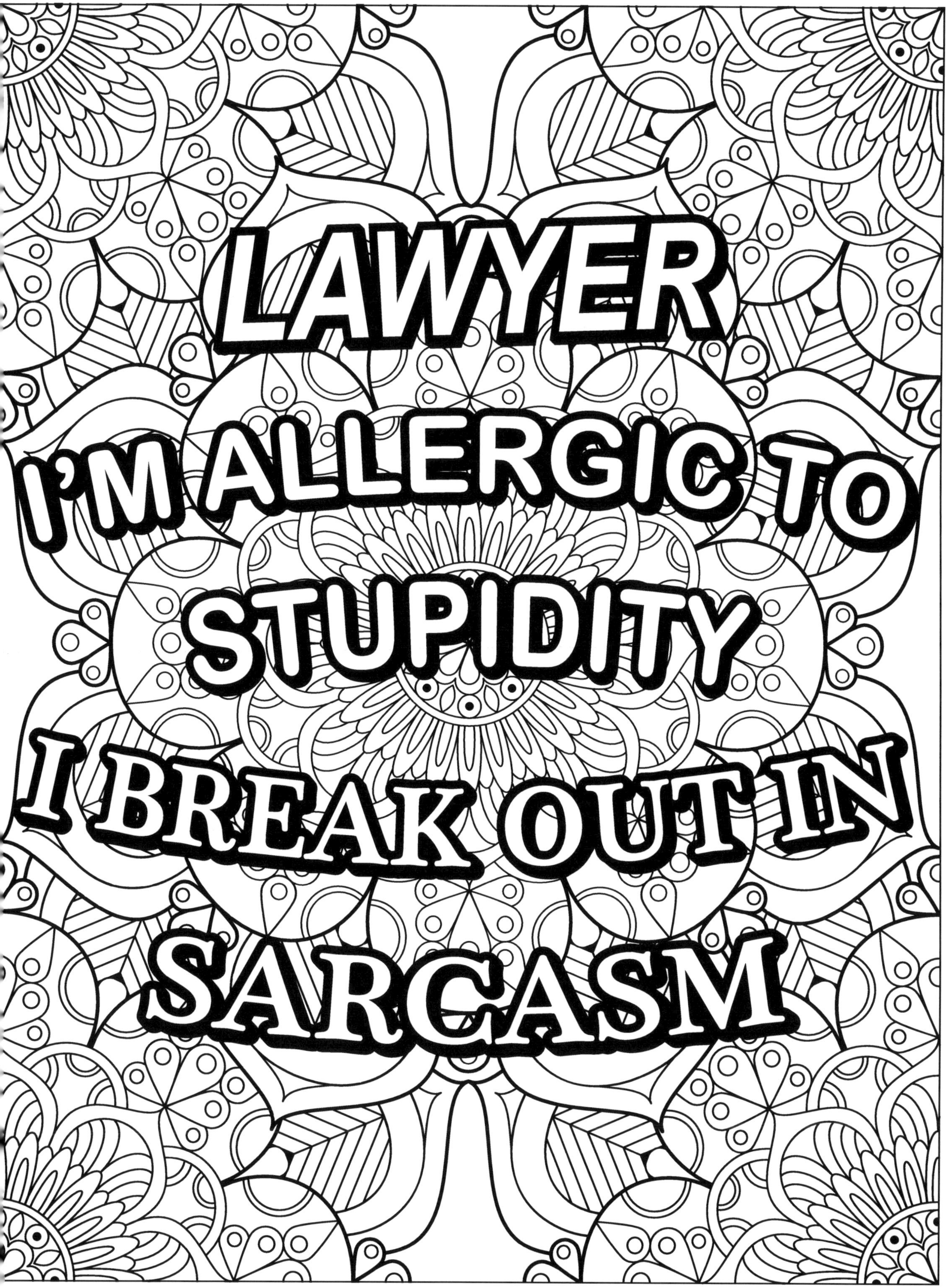
LAWYER
I'M ALLERGIC TO
STUPIDITY
I BREAK OUT IN
SARCASM

PLEASE DON'T
CONFUSE YOUR
GOOGLE SEARCH
WITH MY
LAW DEGREE

INNOCENT
UNTILL I
PROVE YOU
GUILTY

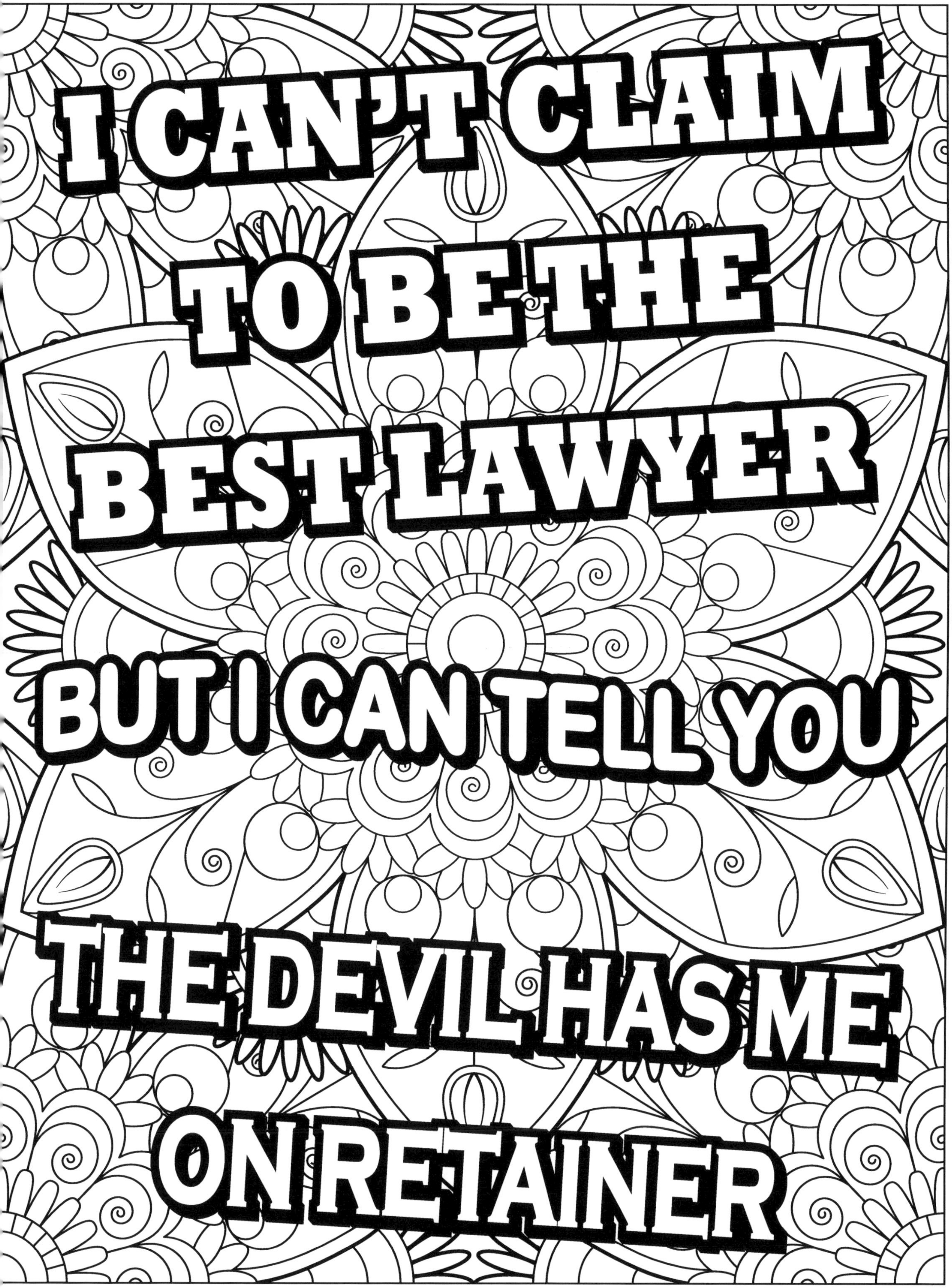
I CAN'T CLAIM
TO BE THE
BEST LAWYER
BUT I CAN TELL YOU
THE DEVIL HAS ME
ON RETAINER

I SEE
GUILTY
PEOPLE

I NEVER DREAMED
I WOULD BE
A SUPER COOL
LAWYER
BUT HERE I AM
Killing It

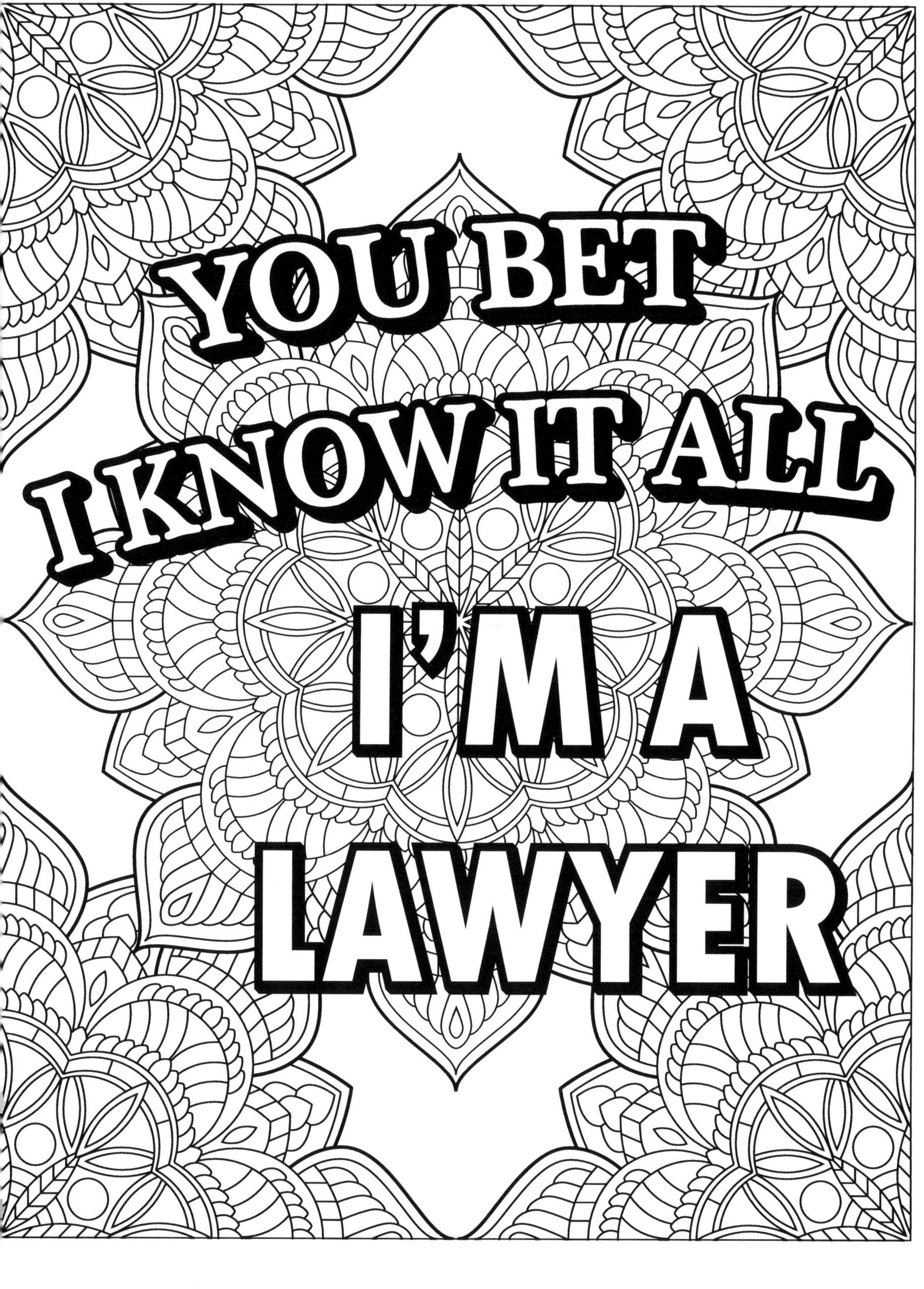
YOU BET
I KNOW IT ALL
I'M A
LAWYER

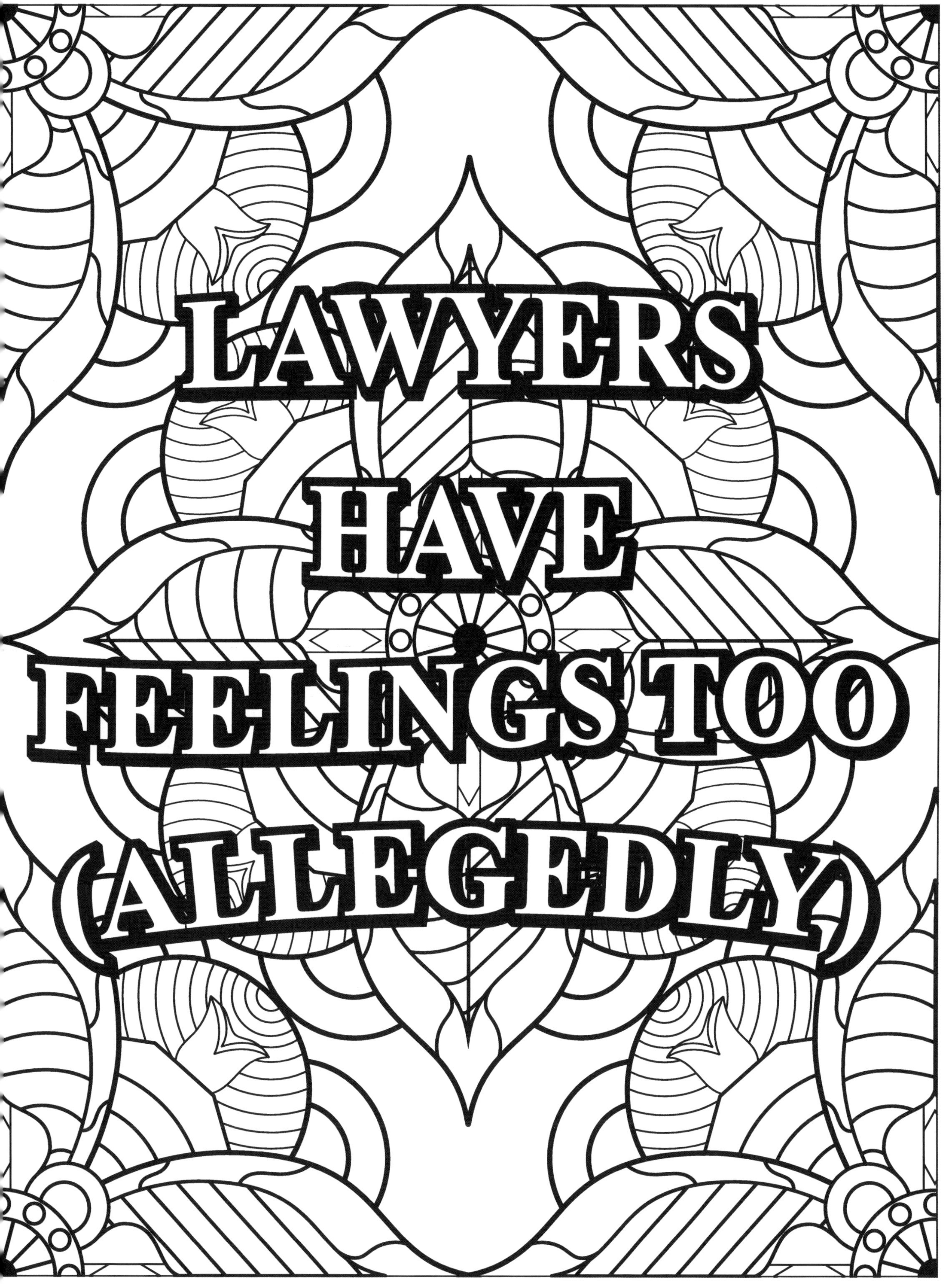
LAWYERS
HAVE
FEELINGS TOO
(ALLEGEDLY)

I'M A
LAWYER
BECAUSE
BADASS
MIRACLE WORKER
ISN'T AN OFFICIAL
JOB TITLE

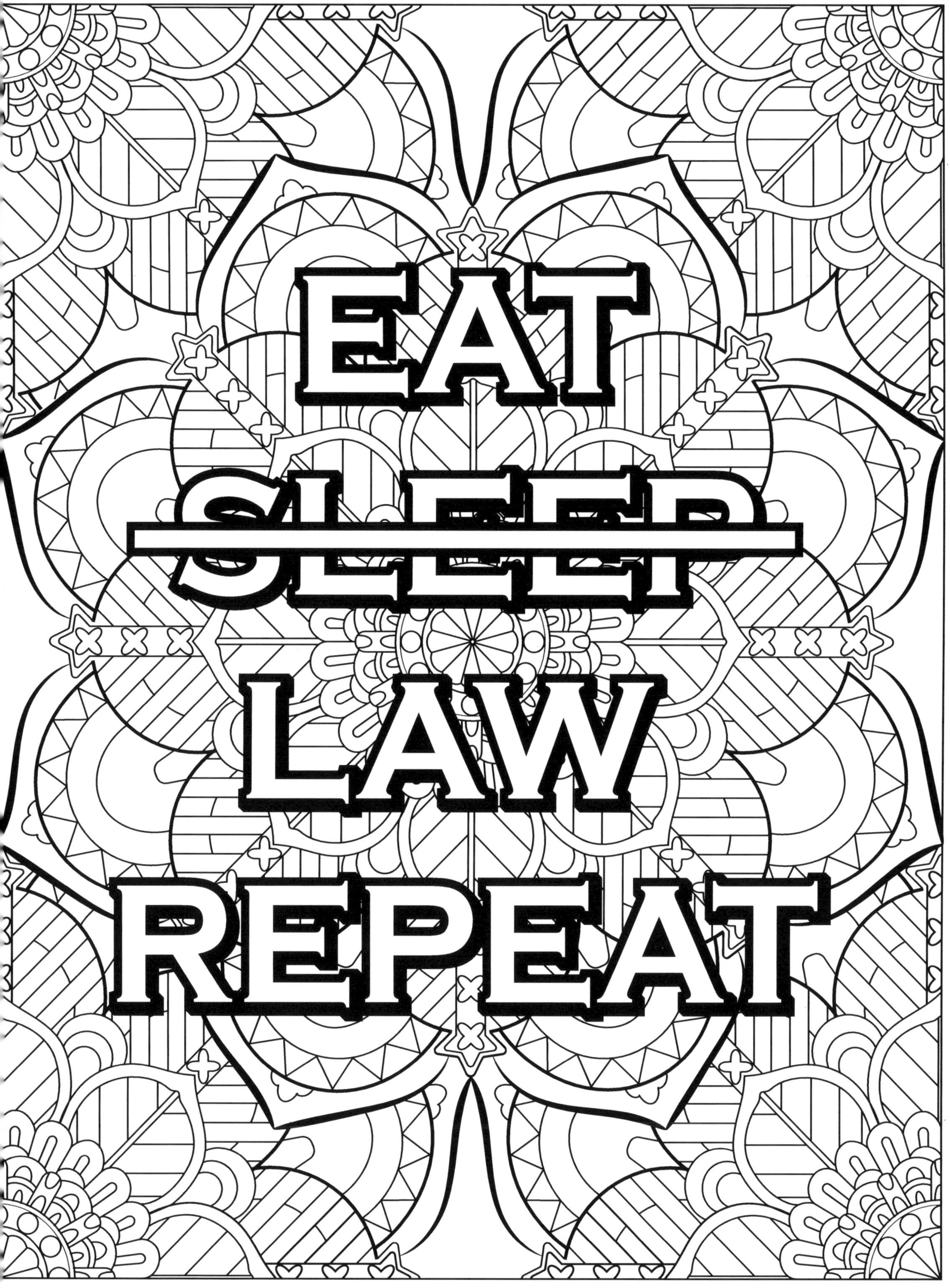
EAT
~~SLEEP~~
LAW
REPEAT

TRUST ME
I'M A
LAWYER

I READ
THE RULES
SO YOU
DON'T HAVE TO

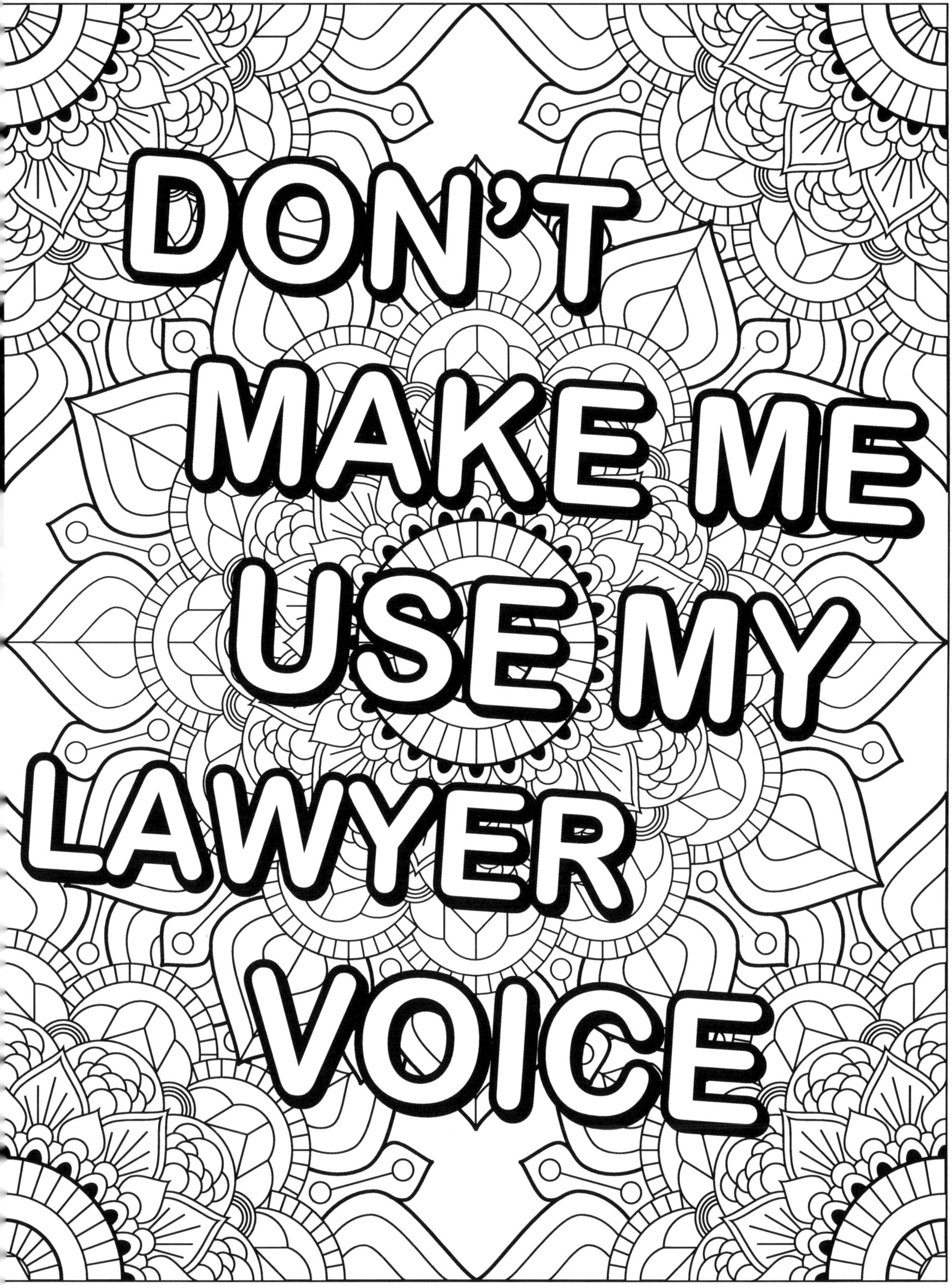
DON'T
MAKE ME
USE MY
LAWYER
VOICE

Color Charts Test

Made in the USA
Middletown, DE
03 December 2019

79849410R00031